CAMBRIDGE PRIMARY
Science

Challenge

6

T0159742

Fiona Baxter and Liz Dilley

CAMBRIDGE
UNIVERSITY PRESS

University Printing House, Cambridge CB2 8BS, United Kingdom

One Liberty Plaza, 20th Floor, New York, NY 10006, USA

477 Williamstown Road, Port Melbourne, VIC 3207, Australia

4843/24, 2nd Floor, Ansari Road, Daryaganj, Delhi – 110002, India

79 Anson Road, #06–04/06, Singapore 079906

Cambridge University Press is part of the University of Cambridge.

It furthers the University's mission by disseminating knowledge in the pursuit of education, learning and research at the highest international levels of excellence.

www.cambridge.org
Information on this title: www.cambridge.org/ 9781316611210

First published 2016

20 19 18 17 16 15 14 13 12 11 10 9 8 7

Produced for Cambridge University Press by
White-Thomson Publishing
www.wtpub.co.uk

Editor: Sonya Newland
Designer: Clare Nicholas

Printed in Spain by GraphyCems

A catalogue record for this publication is available from the British Library

ISBN 978-1-316-61121-0 Paperback

Additional resources for this publication at www.cambridge.org/

Cover artwork: Bill Bolton

....

Contents

Introduction

This series of primary science activity books complements *Cambridge Primary Science* and progresses, through practice, learner confidence and depth of knowledge in the skills of scientific enquiry (SE) and key scientific vocabulary and concepts. These activity books will:

- enhance and extend learners' scientific knowledge and facts
- promote scientific enquiry skills and learning in order to think like a scientist
- advance each learner's knowledge and use of scientific vocabulary and concepts in their correct context.

The *Challenge* activity books extend learners' understanding of the main curriculum, providing an opportunity to increase the depth of their knowledge and scientific enquiry skills from a key selection of topics. This workbook is offered as extension to the main curriculum and therefore it does not cover all the curriculum framework content for this stage.

How to use the activity books

These activity books have been designed for use by individual learners, either in the classroom or at home. As teachers and as parents, you can decide how and when they are used by your learner to best improve their progress. The *Challenge* activity books target specific topics (lessons) from Grades 1–6 from all the units covered in *Cambridge Primary Science*. This targeted approach has been carefully designed to consolidate topics where help is most needed.

How to use the units

Unit introduction

Each unit starts with an introduction for you as the teacher or parent. It clearly sets out which topics are covered in the unit and the learning objectives of the activities in each section. This is where you can work with learners to select all, most or just one of the sections according to individual needs.

The introduction also provides advice and tips on how best to support the learner in the skills of scientific enquiry and in the practice of key scientific vocabulary.

Sections

Each section matches a corresponding lesson in the main series. Sections contain write-in activities that are supported by:

- Key words – key vocabulary for the topic, also highlighted in bold in the sections
- Key facts – a short fact to support the activities where relevant
- Look and learn – where needed, activities are supported with scientific exemplars for extra support of how to treat a concept or scientific method
- Remember – tips for the learner to steer them in the right direction.

How to approach the write-in activities

Teachers and parents are advised to provide students with a blank A5 notebook at the start of each grade for learners to use alongside these activity books. Most activities will provide enough space for the answers required. However, some learner responses – especially to enquiry-type questions – may require more space for notes. Keeping notes and plans models how scientists work and encourages learners to explore and record their thinking, leaving the activity books for the final, more focused answers.

Think about it questions

Each unit also contains some questions for discussion at home with parents, or at school. Although learners will record the outcomes of their discussions in the activity book, these questions are intended to encourage the students to think more deeply.

Self-assessment

Each section in the unit ends with a self-assessment opportunity for learners: empty circles with short learning statements. Teachers or parents can ask learners to complete the circles in a number of ways, depending on their age and preference, e.g. with faces, traffic light colours or numbers. The completed self-assessments provide teachers with a clearer understanding of how best to progress and support individual learners.

Glossary of key words and concepts

At the end of each activity book there is a glossary of key scientific words and concepts arranged by unit. Learners are regularly reminded to practise saying these words out loud and in sentences to improve communication skills in scientific literacy.

1 Humans and animals

What learners will practise and reinforce

The activities in this Challenge unit give learners further practice in the following topics in the Learner's Book and Activity Book:

Topic	In this topic, learners will:
1.1 Body organs	see Skills Builder, Section 1.1
1.2 The heart	explain how the heart works
1.4 The lungs and breathing	see Skills Builder, Section 1.4
1.5 The digestive system	make a model of the digestive system
1.6 What do the kidneys do?	answer questions about the kidneys
1.7 What does the brain do?	draw a graph of brain growth

Help your learner

In this unit, learners will practise using graphs to present results (Section 1.7). They will also practise using results to draw a conclusion and make further predictions (Section 1.7). To help them:

1 Explain that the scale on a line graph must be divided into equal intervals — for example five or ten years, or 100 g or 200 g.

TEACHING TIP

Talk about ways to keep the body organs healthy, such as following a balanced diet, drinking six to eight glasses of water every day and doing regular exercise.

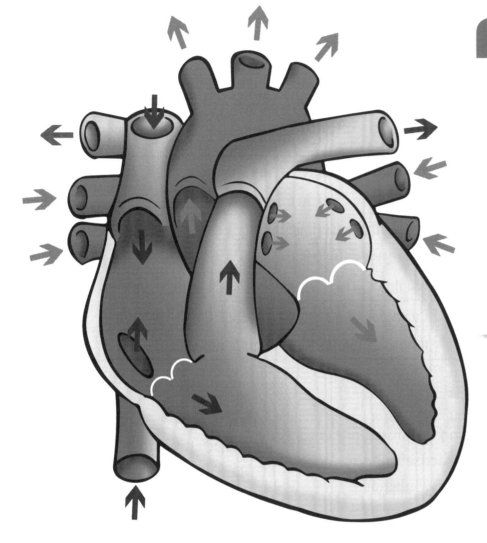

KEY FACT

The **heart** is sometimes called a 'double pump'. This is because the right side of the heart pumps blood to the lungs and the left side of the heart pumps blood to the rest of the body.

Explain the way the heart works

Circle the letter of the correct answer to each of the following questions about the heart.

1 Your heart pumps blood through the body. This process is called ...

   a heartbeat

   b pulsing

   c circulation.

2 The heart is part of the _____ system.

   a organ

   b circulatory

   c blood.

3 The left side of the heart pumps blood that contains ...

   a oxygen

   b no oxygen

   c many different gases.

4 The right side of the heart pumps blood to ...

   a the brain

   b the lungs

   c the kidneys.

5 The **circulatory system** is made up of the ...

   a heart only

   b heart and blood vessels

   c heart, blood vessels and blood.

CHECK YOUR LEARNING

◯ I know about the heart and its functions.

Make a model digestive system

Resources

You will need materials such as plastic bottles, plastic tubing, plastic bags, balloons, string, paper cups, cardboard tubes, a bicycle inner tube, old pantyhose (tights), scissors, elastic bands and electrical tape.

1 Design and make a model of the **digestive system.** Your model should:

- be made of everyday or waste materials
- show the parts of the digestive system in the correct order.

Place your completed model on a piece of cardboard or hardboard. You can use glue or sticky putty to hold it in place.

Use your model to explain to a family member or friend how the digestive system works.

Remember:

Think about the structure and the function of each part of the digestive system – for example the gullet is a long, narrow tube. This will help you choose the best materials for the different parts.

2 Think about it!

What other **organs** are needed for digestion?
Find out about them and add one or two to your model.

CHECK YOUR LEARNING

◯ I can make a model of the digestive system from everyday materials.

◯ I know the order of the organs in the digestive system.

◯ I can explain the way the digestive system works.

1.6 What do the kidneys do?

Find out about the kidneys and liver

Read the information about the **kidneys** and **liver**, then answer the questions.

The kidneys do some important jobs, which help to keep your body working well. They **filter** the blood to remove waste products. These leave the body in the **urine**. The kidneys also keep the right volume of fluid in the body. The blood is filtered through the kidneys many times a day. The kidneys remove excess fluid from the blood. If the volume of fluid in your body goes down (for example if you **sweat** a lot or you are not drinking enough water), your kidneys will not make much urine until the amount of fluid in your body goes up. You can look after your kidneys by drinking six to eight glasses of water each day.

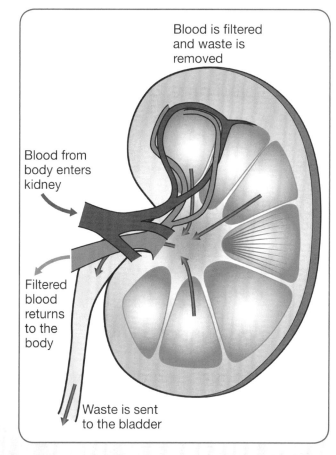

Blood is filtered and waste is removed

Blood from body enters kidney

Filtered blood returns to the body

Waste is sent to the bladder

Your liver is the heaviest organ inside your body. By the time you are grown up, your liver will be about the size of a football and will weigh about 1.4 kg. The liver does over 500 jobs in the body. The liver's main job is to take **toxins** out of your blood and break them down. Toxins are harmful substances that can damage the body – for example alcohol and drugs. The liver produces an important liquid called **bile**. Bile helps you digest fats. It also stores energy for the body.

1 Describe two jobs that the kidneys do in the body.

_____

_____

2 a What liquid do the kidneys produce?

_____

b If you drink a lot of tea on cold day, how will it affect the volume of this liquid that the kidneys produce?

_____

3 Write down a word from the information that means the same as:

liquid _____

poisons _____

the amount of a liquid _____

4 Which function of the liver is similar to a function of the kidneys?

_____

5 Suggest two things that people can do to keep their livers healthy.

_____

_____

CHECK YOUR LEARNING

◯ I know what the kidneys do in the body.

◯ I know what the liver does in the body.

1.7 What does the brain do?

LOOK AND LEARN

At birth, the **brain** is about one-quarter of its full adult size. By the age of two, the brain is almost three times bigger than at birth. During the first two years of your life, lots of connections develop in your brain as you learn to do things such as recognise people, sit, crawl, walk, talk, use a spoon and drink from a cup. By the age of six, your brain is 95% of its adult weight.

Draw a graph of brain growth

This table shows the average size of the brain in males and females of different ages.

Age	Male brain size (g)	Female brain size (g)
birth	380	360
1 year	970	940
2 years	1120	1040
3 years	1270	1090
6 years	1370	1200
11 years	1440	1260
20 years	1450	1310
60 years	1370	1250
80 years	1310	1190

Remember:

The brain cannot repair itself. If any part of the brain is damaged, it cannot regrow.

1 Draw a line graph to show brain growth. Use different coloured lines for males and females.

2 Between which ages does the brain grow the most? Suggest a reason for this.

_____

_____

_____

3 Compare the brain size of males and females. Who has the bigger brain? Suggest a reason for this.

_____

_____

_____

4 At what age does the brain stop growing?

_____

5 **Think about it!**

Why do you think the brain gets smaller as people start
to get old?

_____

_____

_____

_____

CHECK YOUR LEARNING

◯ I can draw a line graph of results.

◯ I can obtain information about brain growth from results.

2 Living things in the environment

What learners will practise and reinforce

The activities in this Challenge unit give learners further practice in the following topics in the Learner's Book and Activity Book:

Topic	In this topic, learners will:
2.1 Food chains in a local habitat	see Skills Builder, Section 2.1
2.2 Food chains begin with plants	see Skills Builder, Section 2.2
2.3 Consumers in food chains	see Skills Builder, Section 2.3
2.4 Food chains in different habitats	identify food chains in a sea turtle habitat
2.5 Deforestation	find out about deforestation in Borneo
2.6 Air pollution	answer questions about air pollution
2.7 Acid rain	find out how acid rain affects Indonesia
2.8 Recycling	see Skills Builder, Section 2.8
2.9 Take care of your environment	identify ways to care for the environment

Help your learner

In this unit, learners will make predictions using scientific understanding (Sections 2.4 and 2.5), identify patterns in results (Section 2.5), create a bar chart (Section 2.7), identify factors that are relevant to a particular situation (Section 2.6) and make relevant observations (Section 2.9). To help them:

1 Make sure learners understand the case studies in Sections 2.5 and 2.7. Discuss each example of the ways in which people are having a negative or positive effect on the environment.

2 Guide learners in choosing a suitable scale for the axes when creating graphs.

habitat, producers,
predator, prey, food chains

Identify food chains in the sea turtle habitat.

Look at the diagram of the sea turtle's **habitat**.

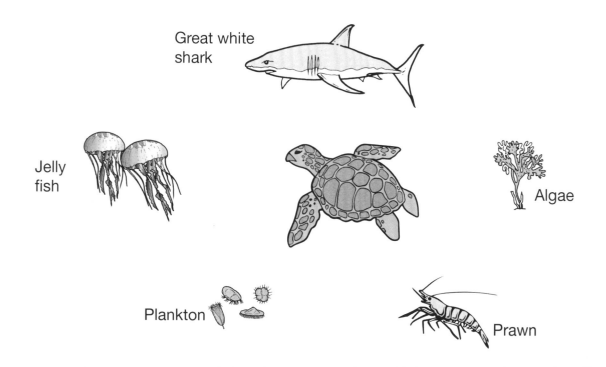

1 Plankton and algae are the **producers** in the sea turtle's habitat. Jellyfish eat plankton and prawns eat algae. Draw a food chain to show each of these feeding relationships.

_____

_____

2 The sea turtle eats jellyfish and prawns.

   a Which animal is the **predator?**

   _____

   b Which animals are the **prey?**

   _____

3 Which of these **food chains** is correct?

   a Jellyfish ⟶ sea turtle

   b Plankton ⟶ jellyfish ⟶ sea turtle

4 Explain your answer to Question 3.

_____

_____

_____

5 The great white shark eats the sea turtle.

   a Which animal is the predator?

   _____

   b Which animal is the prey?

   _____

   c Draw a food chain to show this feeding relationship. Remember to start with the producer.

   _____

5 Think about it!

Predict what would happen to the sea turtles if all the great white sharks disappeared from this habitat.

_____

_____

_____

_____

CHECK YOUR LEARNING

○ I can identify producers, predators and prey in a habitat.

○ I can draw a food chain.

○ I can make a prediction using scientific knowledge and understanding.

Deforestation in Borneo

Read the information about deforestation in Borneo, then answer the questions.

Borneo is the largest island in Asia. The northern part is Malaysian and the southern part is Indonesian. The tropical forests of Borneo are home to thousands of plant and animal **species**: 5000 species of flowering plants and 3000 species of trees; 221 species of mammals and 420 species of birds.

Unfortunately, many of Borneo's animal and plant species, such as orang-utans, are becoming **endangered** or even **extinct**. This is because their rainforest habitat is disappearing. For the last 70 years, deforestation has destroyed much of it. Most of the trees are cut down to make furniture and other products. The wood is mainly exported to China.

Many trees are destroyed to make way for crops, especially oil palm plantations. Palm oil is the most commonly used vegetable oil in the world.

Recently, some of the forest has been destroyed by fires. This is because as the forests become less dense they become drier, so they catch fire more easily.

1 **What is the natural vegetation in Borneo?**

_____

2 Describe two ways in which humans are having a negative effect on the natural vegetation.

_____

_____

3 **a** What is the difference between an endangered animal and an extinct animal?

_____

_____

_____

b What is causing animals to become endangered or extinct in Borneo?

_____

4 Look at the maps of Borneo showing the areas covered by tropical forest.

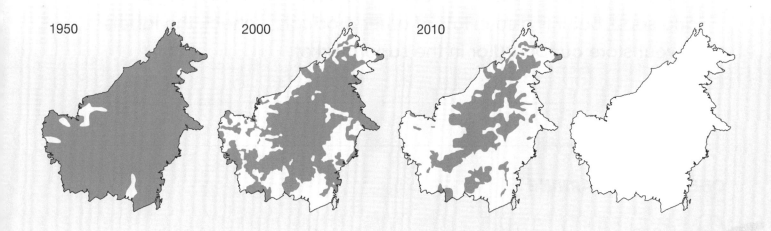

1950   2000   2010

a What does the 1950 map show?

_____

_____

_____

b Is deforestation increasing or decreasing? What tells you this?

_____

_____

_____

c Predict what will happen in the future, then shade in the forested area on the last map to show your prediction for 2050.

_____

_____

5 Think about it!

Find out how much palm oil your family uses. It is in cooking oil and soap, but it is also in lots of other products – check the labels in your store cupboard or in the supermarket.

_____

_____

CHECK YOUR LEARNING

◯ I can explain how deforestation is harming the environment.

◯ I can make a prediction based on evidence.

2.6 Air pollution

Explain the causes and effects of air pollution

1 Match the words relating to **air pollution** with their definitions.

bronchitis	a substance that causes pollution
carbon monoxide	a lung infection that can be caused by polluted air
pollutant	a poisonous gas given off when coal and oil are burnt
sulfur dioxide	an allergic reaction that makes it hard to breathe
asthma	a poisonous gas in car exhaust

2 Name three types of energy that cause less pollution than burning coal and oil.

_____

_____

_____

3 Give two reasons why these types of energy are not used more widely.

_____

_____

4 Complete the following sentences to describe air pollution in the area where you live.

a In my area, the main pollutants are ...

_____

_____

_____

b The main causes of pollution are ...

_____

_____

_____

c Some of the effects of pollution in my area are ...

_____

_____

_____

5 Think about it!

At what time of year is air pollution worst where you live? Why do you think this is?

_____

_____

_____

CHECK YOUR LEARNING

◯ I can describe the causes and effects of air pollution where I live.

LOOK AND LEARN

The **pH** measurement system is used to show how acidic a liquid is. The pH scale is 0–14. The lower the pH, the more acidic the liquid is. Rainwater normally has a pH level of 5.6. Rainwater with a pH level below 5.6 is **acid rain**.

Acid rain in Indonesia

Read the information about the effects of acid rain in Indonesia, then answer the questions.

Rainwater falling in Indonesia may appear clean, but it contains dangerous levels of **pollutants**. These can harm the environment and people's health.

Scientists researched the average pH level of rainwater in four major cities in Indonesia over one year. In Jakarta the pH was 4.5, in Manado it was 4.2, in Pontianak it was 4.3 and in Bogor it was 4.4. So in all four cities rainwater was acidic.

Many people in big cities such as Jakarta do not have piped water. They drink water from rainwater tanks or rivers. This acidic water is harmful to drink.

Acid rain pouring into the oceans could damage coral and fish. In western Indonesia, acid rain is making the soil less fertile, so crops do not grow so well.

Indonesia needs to take actions to stop acid rain by keeping checks on air-pollution levels.

1 What is acid rain?

_____

_____

2 **a** What does the rain in Jakarta contain?

_____

b Why are these dangerous?

_____

_____

3 Name three harmful effects of acid rain in Indonesia.

_____

_____

_____

4 Record the pH level of rainwater in the four Indonesian cities in a table.

Remember:

Think about what headings you should give each column in your table

5 Draw a bar chart to show the pH level of rainwater in the four Indonesian cities.

6 **Think about it!**

Name some other effects of acid rain besides those mentioned in the case study.

_____

_____

_____

CHECK YOUR LEARNING

○ I can use my knowledge of science to understand a case study about acid rain.

○ I can show data on a bar chart.

2.9 Take care of your environment

Identify good and bad effects on the environment

Look at the pictures in the boxes below. They show some different ways that people affect the environment.

1 Draw a cross on the pictures that show *negative effects* on the environment. Fill in the gaps in the sentences beneath these boxes. Choose words from the box below.

2 Draw a tick on the pictures that show a way of *caring* for the environment. Fill in the gaps in the sentences beneath these boxes. Choose the words from the box below.

rinse	holes	shower	pollute
germs	litter	waste	
less	buses	save	

1 Put your _____ in the bin.

2 Flies leave _____ which can make you sick. Keep food and eating areas clean.

3 Use _____ water in the bath. If possible _____ instead.

4 _____ water – turn on the tap only when you need to _____ your teeth.

5 Walking or cycling does not _____ the environment like cars or _____.

6 Check that your hosepipe does not have _____ along the pipe which will _____ water.

3 Draw pictures of two more ways to care for your environment in the two empty boxes. Write a sentence underneath each box.

7 _____

8 _____

_____

_____

_____

_____

CHECK YOUR LEARNING

◯   I can identify and describe how to take care of the environment.

3 Material changes

The activities in this Challenge unit give learners further practice in the following topics in the Learner's Book and Activity Book:

Topic	In this topic, learners will:
3.1 Reversible and irreversible changes	see Skills Builder, Section 3.1
3.2 Mixing and separating solids	separate pins from a mixture of flour and pins
3.3 Soluble and insoluble substances	see Skills Builder, Section 3.3
3.4 Separating insoluble substances	see Skills Builder, Section 3.4
3.5 Solutions	use the particle model to explain how substances dissolve
3.6 Making solids dissolve faster	identify and explain factors that affect dissolving
3.7 Grain size and dissolving	complete a report on an investigation about dissolving

Help your learner

In this unit, learners will practise making predictions (Sections 3.2, 3.5, 3.6 and 3.7) and making relevant observations (Section 3.2). They will also choose what evidence to collect and which equipment to use (Sections 3.5 and 3.7) and use results to draw a conclusion (Section 3.7). To help them:

1 Remind learners that when they choose equipment for an investigation, they must make sure it is suitable for what they are testing.

TEACHING TIP

Remind learners about the particle model, explaining that we use shapes to represent particles that we cannot see in real life.

mixture, separate

Separate pins from rice

Resources
You will need a jar with a lid, rice, pins, a sheet of paper and a magnet.

Remember:
In a mixture, the substances are not chemically joined.

Put the rice and pins in the jar. Shake well.

1 Using your scientific knowledge, explain why you know this is a **mixture**.

_____

_____

_____

Pour your mixture from the jar onto the sheet of paper.

2 Predict what will happen if you hold a magnet above your mixture.

_____

_____

Test your prediction.

3 Describe what happened and explain why.

_____

_____

_____

4 Describe a method to **separate** these mixtures:

a Raisins and currants.

_____

_____

_____

b Couscous and flour.

_____

_____

_____

CHECK YOUR LEARNING

◯ I know that some magnetic solids can be separated from a mixture by using a magnet.

Use the particle model to explain solutions

LOOK AND LEARN

Scientists often use a **scientific model** to explain how and why something happens. The **particle** model says that all matter is made up of particles. In real life we can't see these particles, but in the model we show them as balls or shapes. We can use the particle model to explain **solutions**.

Resources
You will need a glass of water, a teaspoon and some sugar.

Mix a teaspoonful of sugar into the glass of water to make a solution. Stir the sugar until it disappears.

1 **a** Where has the sugar gone?

_____

b What can you do to test whether the sugar is still in the water?

_____

c What is the sugar in the solution called?

_____

d What is the water in the solution called?

_____

We can represent particles of water and particles of sugar in a model like this:

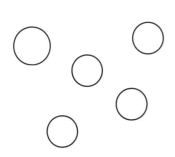

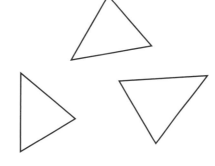

Particles of water   Particles of sugar

2 Using the particle model, draw a picture of the solution you made. Label your particles.

Add more sugar to your solution, one teaspoonful at a time. Stir after you have added each teaspoon of sugar. Keep dissolving teaspoons of sugar until the sugar stops dissolving. At this point, we call the solution a **saturated** solution.

3 **a** How many teaspoons of sugar did you dissolve to get a saturated solution?

_____

b Using the particle model, draw a picture of your saturated solution. Label your particles.

4 **Think about it!**

What can you do to make more sugar dissolve in your saturated solution without adding more water? Explain why this will work.

_____

_____

_____

CHECK YOUR LEARNING

◯ I can explain solutions using a scientific model.

3.6 Making solids dissolve faster

Identify factors that make sugar dissolve

Mrs Pather poured a cup of tea from the teapot and added two teaspoons of sugar. The tea was not very hot so she drank it quickly. As she drank the last few drops, she noticed there was still sugar in the bottom of the cup.

1 Why was there still sugar at the bottom of the cup?

_____

_____

2 What two things could Mrs Pather have done to make all the sugar **dissolve**?

_____

_____

3 Use your knowledge of particles to explain why these two actions helped the sugar dissolve faster.

_____

_____

_____

_____

4 a Predict what would happen to the sugar if Mrs Pather forgot to drink her cup of tea and left it standing for the whole afternoon.

_____

_____

b Explain your prediction.

_____

_____

_____

_____

Remember:

A prediction is what you think will happen based on your scientific knowledge or observations. It is not a guess.

CHECK YOUR LEARNING

◯ I can identify and explain factors that affect dissolving.

◯ I can make and explain a prediction.

3.7 Grain size and dissolving

Complete a report on dissolving

Gina takes a vitamin tablet every morning just before she leaves for school. The tablet dissolves in water. Sometimes she nearly misses her bus because she has to wait for the tablet to dissolve.

Gina has an idea that smaller pieces will dissolve faster. To test her idea, Gina cuts two vitamin tablets into smaller pieces. She dissolves the pieces of each tablet in a glass of cold water. These are her results:

Number of pieces of tablet	Time for tablet to dissolve (seconds)
1	90
2	45
4	25

KEY FACT

The **rate** of dissolving depends on how much contact there is between the particles of the solute and the solvent. If the solute is made up of one large particle, there is only one surface across which the solute can mix with the solvent particles and dissolve. This makes dissolving slower. If the solute is made up of lots of small particles, they have lots of small surfaces that are in contact with the solvent, so they dissolve faster.

1 Gina wrote a report on her investigation. Fill in the spaces on her report.

Aim: I am going to investigate the effect of _____ on dissolving.

I will need the following apparatus:

_____

_____

_____

_____

Things I will keep the same are:

_____

_____

_____

I will change:

_____

I will measure:

_____

_____

My prediction is that the <u>whole tablet/2 tablet pieces/4 tablet pieces/all the tablets</u> will dissolve <u>faster/slower/at the same rate</u>.

My conclusion is that:

_____

_____

2 Why did Gina use a whole tablet as well as smaller pieces of tablets?

_____

_____

_____

3 **a** Predict the length of time a crushed vitamin tablet will take to dissolve. Add your prediction to the results table.

b Use your knowledge about dissolving to explain your prediction.

_____

_____

_____

_____

CHECK YOUR LEARNING

◯ I can plan an investigation.

◯ I can identify factors that affect dissolving.

◯ I can draw a conclusion and make further predictions.

4 Forces and motion

What learners will practise and reinforce

The activities in this Challenge unit give learners further practice in the following topics in the Learner's Book and Activity Book:

Topic	In this topic, learners will:
4.1 Mass and weight	see Skills Builder, Section 4.1
4.2 How forces act	see Skills Builder, Section 4.2
4.3 Balanced and unbalanced forces	identify balanced and unbalanced forces
4.4 The effects of forces	see Skills Builder, Section 4.4
4.5 Forces and energy	identify and explain when work is being done
4.6 Friction	explain why some shoes grip the ground better than others
4.7 Investigating friction	investigate friction in liquids
4.8 Air resistance and drag	see Skills Builder, Section 4.8

Help your learner

In this unit, learners will practise making observations using simple apparatus, using results to draw conclusions and identifying factors that are relevant to the situation (Section 4.7). They will also identify a pattern in results (Section 4.6). To help them:

1 Explain that a pattern is usually a regular or predictable change in the results due to a change in the factor being investigated. For example a marble will roll shorter and shorter distances on a surface as the roughness of surface increases.

TEACHING TIP

Learners can test how well different shoes grip the ground themselves by attaching an elastic band to the shoe and measuring how much the elastic band stretches before the shoes moves.

4.3 Balanced and unbalanced forces

balanced, unbalanced

Identify balanced and unbalanced forces

Mr Strong has to move a heavy crate.

1 Draw arrows on the picture to show the direction of the forces acting on the crate.

Remember:

Forces act in pairs that work in opposite directions.

2 The crate exerts a bigger force than Mr Thomson exerts. Will the crate move?

_____

3 Mr Thomson's friend comes to help him push the crate. In what way do you think the movement of the crate will change when there are two people pushing it? Explain your answer.

_____

_____

_____

CHECK YOUR LEARNING

◯ I can identify the direction in which forces act.

◯ I can explain why increasing force changes the movement of an object.

4.5 Forces and energy

LOOK AND LEARN

We use the word 'work' in everyday life. For example we say that we work hard at school, or that a nurse works in a clinic. In science 'work' means something different. **Work** is when a force makes an object move. The force gives the object energy. A large force on an object will give it more energy and make it move further. The more energy the object has, the more work it can do.

Identify and explain when work is being done

Look at the pictures, then answer the questions.

1 Is work being done? Say why or why not.

_____

_____

_____

2 Is work being done? Say why or why not.

_____

_____

_____

A　　　　　　　　B

3 **a** What force is being exerted?

_____

b On which object is the force exerted?

_____

c In which drawing, A or B, is the object doing more work? Explain why. Use the words 'force', 'energy' and 'move' in your explanation.

_____

_____

_____

CHECK YOUR LEARNING

◯ I can identify and explain when work is being done.

◯ I can recognise and explain when more work is being done.

4.6 Friction

forcemeter, tread, pattern

How well do different shoes grip?

Nor and Aliya tested different shoes to find out how well they gripped the ground. They pulled each shoe along the floor with a **forcemeter** and measured how much force was needed to make the shoe move. They repeated the test twice.

These are their results:

Type of shoe	Force needed to move shoe		
trainer	9N	10N	10N
hiking boot	12N	12N	13N
ballet shoe	3N	2N	3N
slipper	4N	5N	4N
indoor shoe	7N	8N	7N

1 Name the force that makes your shoes grip the ground when you walk.

_____

Remember:

The soles of shoes have **tread** on them to make them grip the ground and stop you from slipping when you walk.

2 Which shoe gripped the ground best? Explain how you know this.

_____

_____

_____

3 Which shoe gripped the ground worst? Explain how you know this.

_____

_____

4 a Which two types of shoe have the smoothest soles with the least tread?

_____

b Which two types of shoe have the roughest soles with the most tread?

_____

c Describe the **pattern** you can see in the results.

_____

_____

d Use your knowledge of forces to explain the pattern.

_____

_____

_____

5 Think about it!

Ballet dancers rub the soles and toes of their ballet shoes in a sticky powder called rosin. Why do they do this this?

_____

_____

CHECK YOUR LEARNING

◯ I can evaluate repeated results.

◯ I can use my knowledge of science to explain why some shoes grip the ground better than others.

Investigate friction in liquids

Resources
You will need three small identical drinking glasses or 200 ml measuring cylinders, a measuring jug, water, dishwashing liquid, two identical coins, modelling clay strips, scissors and a ruler.

Remember:
Long, narrow glasses are best for this investigation if you do not have measuring cylinders. Don't waste the dishwashing liquid after your investigation – use it to wash the dishes!

Put **200 ml of water** in one glass and **200 ml of dishwashing liquid** into another glass.

Drop a coin into each glass at the same time.

1 **a** In which glass does the coin reach the bottom first?

_____

b In which liquid is **friction** the greatest? Explain how you know this.

_____

_____

_____

Put 200 ml of dishwashing liquid into the third glass. Remove the coin from the other glass of dishwashing liquid so you have two glasses.

Cut two 1 cm long pieces from a strip of modelling clay.

Roll one piece of modelling clay into a ball. Roll the other piece into a sausage shape.

Drop each modelling clay shape at the same time into a glass of dishwashing liquid.

2 **a** Which one reaches the bottom first? Suggest a reason for this observation.

_____

_____

_____

b Why is it important to use pieces of modelling clay of the same size to make the shapes?

_____

_____

_____

3 Write a conclusion about factors you have observed that affect friction in liquids.

_____

_____

_____

4 Which liquids create the most friction? Try out different liquids to find out. Remember to keep your test fair.

_____

_____

_____

KEY FACT

Friction is a force that slows down movement between surfaces. In liquids, friction is called **drag**. Although liquids slow down objects moving through them, they also make surfaces smoother and reduce friction between two solids rubbing together.

CHECK YOUR LEARNING

◯ I can make observations using simple apparatus.

◯ I can use results to draw a conclusion.

5 Electrical conductors and insulators

The activities in this Challenge unit give learners further practice in the following topics in the Learner's Book and Activity Book:

Topic	In this topic, learners will:
5.1 Which materials conduct electricity?	see Skills Builder, Section 5.1
5.2 Does water conduct electricity?	find out about the dangers of lightning and water
5.3 Do different metals conduct electricity equally well?	learn about semiconductors
5.4 Choosing the right materials for electrical appliances	see Skills Builder, Section 5.4
5.5 Circuit symbols	see Skills Builder, Section 5.5
5.6 Changing the number of components	predict and test the effect of changes to a circuit
5.7 Adding different components	see Skills Builder, Section 5.7
5.8 Length and thickness of wire in a circuit	look at a case study showing the benefits of scientific knowledge
5.9 How scientists invented batteries	discover how scientists have created batteries for different purposes

Help your learner

In this unit, learners will practise making predictions (Sections 5.2 and 5.8) and choosing what evidence to collect and saying whether the evidence supports their predictions (Section 5.6). They will also consider how scientists have suggested new ideas (Sections 5.3 and 5.9). To help them:

1 Read the case studies in this unit with learners and help them with parts they may not understand.

5.2 Does water conduct electricity?

lightning, volts, conductor

Explain the dangers of lightning

KEY FACT

Lightning is electrical energy in the atmosphere. A spark of lightning occurs within a cloud, between clouds, or between a cloud and the ground. Each spark can be over 8 km long. It can reach temperatures hotter than the surface of the Sun and may contain 300 million **volts** of electricity.

Read the information about lightning, then answer the questions.

Lightning does not strike the ocean as much as land. However, when it does, it spreads out over the surface of the water, which acts as a **conductor**.

People on or in water are at risk during thunderstorms. Swimming is particularly dangerous because part of a swimmer's body is out of the water. Lightning always strikes the highest thing available. Surfers and paddle skiers are particularly at risk.

Boats can be fitted with lightning conductors, which direct the electrical charge into the sea. This can prevent people or equipment on the boat from being struck by lightning.

If you are in a house during a lightning storm, you should avoid contact with water. Do not wash your hands, do not take a shower, do not wash dishes or clothes.

1 Why does seawater act as a conductor of electricity?

_____

_____

2 Why are surfers and paddle skiers particularly at risk during a thunderstorm?

_____

_____

3 Why do you think fish are not often killed by lightning?

_____

_____

4 What is a lightning conductor? Explain the way it works.

_____

_____

_____

5 What is the only type of water that does not conduct electricity? Why?

_____

6 Think about it!

Why is it dangerous to swim in a swimming pool during a thunderstorm?

_____

_____

CHECK YOUR LEARNING

◯ I know that most water conducts electricity.

◯ I know ways to be safe during a lightning storm.

5.3 Do different metals conduct electricity equally well?

semiconductors, insulator, elements

Research semiconductors

LOOK AND LEARN

Semiconductors are substances that are in between being a metal and a non-metal. They have the properties of a conductor and the properties of an **insulator**. Computers, tablet devices and smartphones all use semiconductors. Semiconductors are also used to make circuits for many home appliances, such as microwave ovens, televisions sets and refrigerators.

1 Name one metal that conducts electricity well. Name one metal that conducts electricity less well.

_____

_____

2 Name one non-metal material that is often used as an electrical insulator.

_____

Use the internet to answer these questions about semiconductors.

3 Silicon is the most common semiconductor. One area of the world makes huge numbers of silicon chips for computers. The area is called Silicon Valley. Where is it?

_____

4 Name two companies that are the biggest manufacturers of silicon chips in the world.

_____

_____

5 Scientists have discovered other **elements** besides silicon that are semiconductors. Find out the names of some of these elements.

_____

_____

_____

6 List some of the things you use at home that contain semiconductors.

_____

_____

_____

CHECK YOUR LEARNING

◯   I know that some metals conduct electricity better than others.

◯   I know what semiconductors are and how important they are in modern life.

Predict the results of making changes to a circuit

1 Draw the circuit symbols for the components listed in the Resources box.

Resources
You will need a 3 V battery, three bulbs in bulb holders, connecting wire and a switch.

Make a circuit with a 3V battery, two bulbs and a switch.

2 Explain how you will test your circuit.

_____

_____

_____

3 Think of a change you could make to the number of bulbs in your circuit. Complete this sentence to describe what you are going to do:

What will happen if I _____?

4 Predict what will happen if you make this change.

_____

_____

_____

5 Test your prediction. Explain the result you got.

_____

_____

_____

_____

6 Draw a **circuit diagram** of the changed circuit you made.

CHECK YOUR LEARNING

◯ I can predict what will happen if I make changes to a circuit.

◯ I can test a prediction and explain the results.

◯ I can draw a circuit diagram.

The jump leads scam

KEY FACT

Jump leads are used to start a car when the battery is flat. The leads carry a large **current** from a working battery in a car to the flat battery to boost or 'jump start' and make it work.

Read the information, then answer the questions.

Abdul's car won't start. He thinks the battery may be flat. He sees some cheap jump leads on sale at the local garage so he buys them to jump start his car.

That afternoon, Abdul's Uncle Ali comes round in his car. Abdul asks his uncle to help him jump start his car with the new jump leads. They clip the positive **clamp** of the jump leads on the positive **terminals** of the batteries of the two cars. Then they do the same with the negative terminals.

1 Why do they connect the jump leads to the batteries of the two cars?

_____

_____

_____

Uncle Ali starts his car. Abdul tries to start his car, but it still will not start. The cables get very hot. Uncle Ali suggests that they try his own jump leads instead of Abdul's. When they connect Uncle Ali's cables, Abdul's car roars into life!

'Abdul, never buy cheap jump leads! They have to carry a big current. Look at the difference between my set and yours.'

Abdul compares the cables. 'My cables feel much lighter than yours. Mine are longer and look thick. But I can see it's the plastic covering that's thick. The copper wires are thin and yours are thick and heavy.'

2 **Why are Uncle Ali's cables heavier than Abdul's?**

_____

_____

3 **Why do short cables work better than long cables?**

_____

_____

_____

4 **Why do thick copper wires work better than thin ones?**

_____

_____

_____

5 Why did Abdul's jump leads get hot? Why could this be dangerous?

_____

_____

_____

6 Think about it!

Explain how Abdul could check the jump leads before he bought them.

_____

_____

_____

_____

CHECK YOUR LEARNING

◯ I know that the strength of the current changes according to the length and thickness of the wire. I can apply this knowledge to a real life situation.

5.9 How scientists invented batteries

Read about battery discoveries

Read the information about modern batteries, then answer the questions.

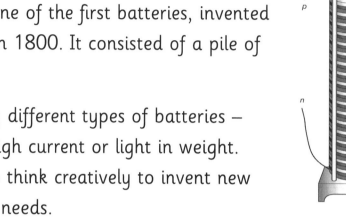

The voltaic pile was one of the first batteries, invented by Alessandro Volta in 1800. It consisted of a pile of copper and zinc discs.

Today there are many different types of batteries – long life, small size, high current or light in weight. Scientists have had to think creatively to invent new batteries for different needs.

Alkaline batteries are used in devices such as torches and toys. You have been using them for your science experiments. Alkaline batteries are cheap and come in different sizes to fit different devices. However, they are not **rechargeable**. This means once they are flat you have to throw them away.

Scientists designed a battery made from a metal called nickel. This battery is called the nickel metal hybride (NiMH) and is rechargeable. The trouble with the NiMH battery is that if it is not used for a long time, its battery power reduces. So scientists went to work to solve this problem.

Swedish scientist Waldmar Jungner invented the nickel cadmium battery (NiCd). Cadmium is a poisonous metal. These batteries can store more energy than the NiMH batteries, but they have a problem with their 'memory'. If they are not fully used up before being recharged, they will not hold as much energy the next time you charge them.

Lithium-ion (Li-ion) batteries have now replaced NiCd batteries. They charge more quickly and weigh much less. They do not suffer 'memory loss' and contain no toxic materials. We use Li-ion batteries in tablets and computers.

1 **Name two advantages of alkaline batteries.**

_____

_____

2 **What advantage does the NiMH battery have over the alkaline battery?**

_____

3 **What advantage does a NiCd battery have over a NiMH battery?**

_____

_____

4 Give two disadvantages of NiCd batteries.

_____

_____

5 Many hand-held power tools such as electric drills now have Li-ion batteries. Why have these batteries made it easier to use tools like this?

_____

_____

6 **Think about it!**

Many stores have recycling bins for batteries. Why do you think they do this?

_____

_____

_____

_____

CHECK YOUR LEARNING

◯ I know that scientists have combined evidence from observation and measurement with creative thinking to suggest new ideas for batteries.

Answers

1 Humans and animals

1.2

Explain the way the heart works

1 **c** circulation.

2 **b** circulatory.

3 **a** oxygen.

4 **b** the lungs.

5 **c** heart, blood vessels and blood.

1.5

Make a model digestive system

1 Learners' models will depend on the materials they choose. The diagram below is an example of a model of a digestive system made from everyday materials.

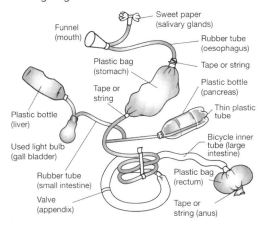

2 **Think about it!**
Other organs include the pancreas, gall bladder, salivary glands, liver.

1.6

Find out about the kidneys and liver

1 The kidneys filter the blood to remove waste products from your body in the urine. Thye balance the volume of fluid in the body.

2 **a** Urine.

b A bigger volume/more urine will be produced.

3 Fluid; toxins; volume.

4 The liver removes harmful substances/toxins from the blood.

5 They should not drink alcohol or use drugs.

1.7

Draw a graph of brain growth

1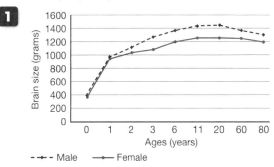

2 Between birth and one year. During this time the baby's body grows quickly and it also learns to do a lot of things, so the brain needs to develop quickly.

3 Males. Males generally have bigger bodies than females so it would be expected that their brains are bigger too.

4 20.

5 **Think about it!**
As we get older, brain cells start to get old and die. They cannot be replaced so the brain gets smaller.

2 Livings things in the environment

2.4

Identify food chains in the sea turtle habitat

1 Plankton → jellyfish.
Algae → prawns.

2 **a** Sea turtle.

b Jellyfish and prawns.

3 Plankton → jellyfish → sea turtle.

4 A food chain must always start with a producer.

5 **a** Great white shark.

b Sea turtle.

c Plankton → jellyfish → sea turtle → great white shark or algae → prawns → sea turtle → great white shark.

6 **Think about it!**
Great white sharks are the predators of the sea turtle, so if they disappeared from the habitat, numbers of sea turtles would increase because no other animals were eating them. However, they would only increase as long as there was enough food for them to eat.

2.5

Deforestation in Borneo

1 Tropical forest.

2 Humans have cut down trees for timber to use for making furniture and other products. They have cut down trees to make room for crops such as palm oil.

3 **a** An endangered animal is one whose numbers have decreased over the years. An extinct animal is one that has died out completely and no longer exists.

b Deforestation is taking away their habitat.

4 **a** Borneo is covered with forest.

b Deforestation is increasing. The maps show a faster increase in deforestation between 2000 and 2010.

c Learners should fill in an area on the 2050 map showing less forest in the area from from the 2010 map. The real pessimist will leave the map blank!

5 **Think about it!**
Learner's own response. They will find palm oil is an ingredient in many food and cleaning products.

2.6

Explain the causes and effects of air pollution

1 bronchitis = a lung infection that can be caused by polluted air.

carbon monoxide = a poisonous gas in car exhaust.

pollutant = a substance that causes pollution.

sulfur dioxide = a poisonous gas given off when coal and oil are burnt.

asthma = an allergic reaction that makes it hard to breathe.

2 Wind power, water power, solar power.

3 They are not as efficient. They are more expensive.

4 Learner's own responses. Likely answers from learners living in cities include:

a In my area, the main pollutants are carbon monoxide, sulfur dioxide and nitrogen oxide.

b The main causes of pollution are cars, buses, trucks and motorcycles giving off exhaust gases and factories burning coal/oil.

c Some of the effects of pollution in my area are people get coughs, asthma, bronchitis and other lung infections.

Likely answers if learners live in the countryside include:

a In my area, the main pollutant is smoke.

b The main causes of pollution are from burning fields/forest/animal manure.

c Some of the effects of pollution in my area are people get coughs, asthma, bronchitis and other lung infections.

5 🄢🄗🄘🄝🄚 🄐🄑🄞🄤🄣 🄘🄣!

Learner's own response.

2.7

Acid rain in Indonesia

1 Acid rain is rainwater with a pH level below 5.6.

2 **a** Pollutants.

b They can harm the environment and people's health.

3 It makes water unsafe to drink. It can damage coral and fish. It can reduce the fertility of the soil.

4

City	pH level
Jakarta	4.5
Manado	4.2
Pontianak	4.3
Bogor	4.4

5

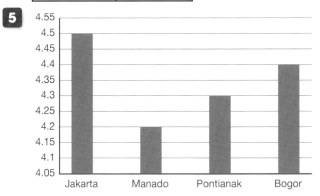

6 🄢🄗🄘🄝🄚 🄐🄑🄞🄤🄣 🄘🄣!

Other effects of acid rain include damage to buildings (wearing away the facades), harming trees and plants, polluting water in rivers and streams and damaging the creatures that live there.

2.9

Identify good and bad effects on the environment

1 Boxes 2, 3, 4 and 6 must have a cross.

2 Boxes 1 and 5 must have a tick.

Sentences under boxes:

1 Put your <u>litter</u> in the bin.

2 Flies leave <u>germs</u> which can make you sick. Keep food and eating areas clean.

3 Use <u>less</u> water in the bath. If possible <u>shower</u> instead.

4 <u>Save</u> water – turn on the tap only when you need to <u>rinse</u> your teeth.

5 Walking or cycling does not <u>pollute</u> the environment like cars or <u>buses</u>.

6 Check that your hosepipe does not have <u>holes</u> along the pipe which will <u>waste</u> water.

3 Suggestions: Save water by never leaving a tap dripping.

Save energy with energy saving bulbs.

Use solar panels to heat water.

Switch off electricity when not using it.

3 Material changes

3.2

Separate pins from rice

1 It consists of two different substances mixed together. The two substances can be separated because they are not chemically joined.

2 The magnet will pick up the pins.

3 The magnet picked up the pins because they are made of steel, which is magnetic. Rice is not magnetic so is not attracted to the magnet.

4 **a** Pick the raisins out with your fingers.

   b Sieve the mixture. The flour will pass through the holes in the sieve and the couscous will remain in the sieve.

3.5

Use the particle model to explain solutions

1 **a** It has dissolved.

   b Taste the water.

   c Solute.

   d Solvent.

2
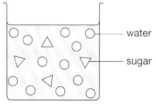

3 **a** Learner's own response. It will depend on how much water is in the glass.

   b
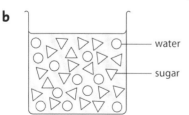

4 Think about it!

Heating the solution will make more sugar dissolve. This is because the particles of water get energy from the heat and move further apart and there is more space for sugar particles.

3.6

Identify factors that make sugar dissolve

1 Because the sugar did not all dissolve.

2 She could have stirred the tea more or heated it up.

3 Stirring moves the particles of solute (sugar) around in the solvent (tea). This allows them to spread more easily into the spaces between the solvent (tea) particles. Heating makes the particles of both solvent and solute move faster. This allows the solute particles to spread more easily into the spaces between the solvent particles until they are evenly spread.

4 **a** The sugar would dissolve.

   b The particles of both the solute (sugar) and solvent (tea) are constantly moving. This makes them bump into each other until they are eventually spread out in the solution. The solute particles can then fit into the spaces between the solvent particles and dissolve.

3.7

Complete a report on dissolving

1 Aim: I am going to investigate the effect of grain size on dissolving.

   I will need the following apparatus:

   water

   vitamin tablets

   glasses/beakers

   stopwatch

   measuring cup

Things I will keep the same are:

type of tablets

volume of water in each glass

temperature of the water

I will change:

the size of the pieces of vitamin tablets.

I will measure:

how long it take different sized-pieces to dissolve.

My prediction is that the 4 tablet pieces will dissolve faster.

OR

My prediction is that the whole tablet will dissolve slower.

My conclusion is that smaller grains of tablet dissolve faster than larger grains of tablet (or similar).

2 She used the whole tablet as a control to compare the results with the results from the cut-up tablets, so she could be sure it was grain size that caused any differences in results.

3 a

Number of pieces of tablet	Time for tablet to dissolve (seconds)
1	90
2	45
4	25
crushed	any range below 10 seconds

b Small grains dissolve faster than large grains. A crushed tablet has lots of very tiny grains so it will dissolve faster because the tiny grains will quickly come into contact with the solvent liquid.

4 Forces and motion

4.3

Identify balanced and unbalanced forces

1

2 No.

3 There will be a bigger force pushing the crate. If the force exerted by two people is bigger than the force exerted by the crate, the crate will move.

4.5

Identify and explain when work is being done

1 No work is being done. The girl and the chair are not moving.

2 Work is being done. The boy is using force to make himself move through the water.

3 a The force exerted is the girl hitting the golf ball.

b The golf ball.

c The object in drawing B is doing more work. It has been hit with more force so it has more energy to make it move further than the object in drawing A.

4.6

How well do different shoes grip?

1 Friction.

2 The hiking boot. It took more force to move the hiking boot than the other shoes.

3 The ballet shoe. It took the least force to move the ballet shoe.

4 **a** The ballet shoe and slipper.

    b The hiking boot and the trainer.

    c The rougher the sole and the more tread it has, the more force it takes to move it.

    d There is more friction between the shoe and the ground if the shoe has a rough sole than if the shoe has a smooth sole. More force is needed to overcome the force of friction to make shoes with rough soles move.

5 **Think about it!**
Ballet shoes have very smooth soles, so rubbing the shoes with rosin increases friction between the shoes and the ground to stop them from slipping on the floor when they dance.

4.7

Investigate friction in liquids

1 **a** The glass of water.

    b The dishwashing liquid. It slows down the movement of the coin through it.

2 **a** The ball of modelling clay reaches the bottom first. The sausage shape does not move through the liquid as easily as the round ball.

    b To make sure the test is fair and compare only the effect of different shapes on friction in liquids. It removes mass as a factor that could affect the results.

3 Friction in liquids is affected by the type of liquid and the shape of the object moving through the liquid.

4 Thick, viscous liquids such as cooking oils, yoghurt (lassi) and glycerine will create more friction than thin liquids like vinegar, milk and cool drinks.

5 Electrical conductors and insulators

5.2

Explain the dangers of lightning

1 Seawater contains dissolved salts, which conduct electricity.

2 Surfers and paddle skiers are standing on their boards above the water, so they are the highest things for lightning to strike.

3 Fish swim under water. When lightning strikes the sea, it spreads out over the surface.

4 A metal spike joined to a cable that leads down to the sea. Lightning strikes the spike and conducts down the cable into the sea. (These are also used on high buildings.)

5 Pure (distilled) water that has been boiled and the steam condensed. There are no salts in the water to conduct the current.

6 **Think about it!**
Swimming-pool water contains chemicals, so this water conducts electricity.

5.3

Research semiconductors

1 Gold, copper and aluminium conduct electricity well. Stainless steel conducts electricity less well.

2 Plastic is often used as an electrical insulator.

3 California, USA.

4 Intel, Samsung, Toshiba or Texas Instruments.

5 Selenium, boron, tellurium, germanium.

6 Computer, tablet, smartphone, TV, microwave, refrigerator.

5.6

Predict the results of making changes to a circuit

1
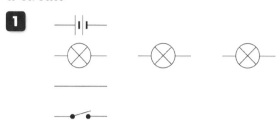

2 Connect everything in the circuit and close the switch. If the bulbs light up the circuit is working.

3 What will happen if I <u>add another bulb to my circuit</u>? Or What will happen if I <u>remove a bulb from my circuit</u>?

4 If you add a third bulb, all three bulbs will glow more dimly.
If you remove a bulb, the remaining bulb will burn more brightly.

5 If a bulb has been added, the bulbs glow more dimly because the 3 V electricity has to be shared between them.
If a bulb has been removed, the remaining bulb will glow more brightly because it has 3 V electricity for a 1.5 V bulb.

6 Circuit with three bulbs:

Circuit with one bulb:

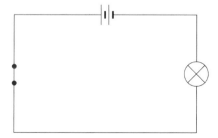

5.8

The jump leads scam

1 They want to send an electric current from the working battery to the flat battery.

2 Because they contain more copper wire.

3 Short cables do not offer as much resistance to the electric current as long cables.

4 Thick copper wires do not offer as much resistance to the electric current as thin cables.

5 When a large current was passed through Abdul's thin cables, they heated up and could have started a fire.

6 **Think about it!**
Abdul could check the jump leads by feeling how heavy they were and also looking at where the copper wire joined on to the crocodile clips to check how thick it was.

5.9

Read about battery discoveries

1 They are cheap and come in different sizes.

2 It is rechargeable.

3 It stores more energy so it does not need to be recharged so often.

4 They have a memory problem and cadmium is a poisonous material.

5 They are lighter in weight, quicker to charge and do not suffer from memory loss.

6 **Think about it!**
Some batteries contain toxic materials such as cadmium and lead, so these have to be disposed of in different ways.

Glossary

1 Humans and animals

bile	a liquid made by the liver that helps break down fats
brain	the organ that controls all body functions
circulatory system	the system formed by the heart, blood vessels and blood to carry food and oxygen around the body
digestive system	the organs needed for the process of digestion, including the stomach and intestines
filter	to let through liquids and dissolved substances but not insoluble substances
heart	a special muscle that pumps blood around the body
kidneys	a pair of bean-shaped organs that filter the blood to remove waste products
liver	the organ in the body that stores energy and breaks down harmful substances
organs	parts of the body that have specific functions to keep us alive
sweat	when drops of water form on the skin to cool it down when our bodies get hot
toxins	harmful substances that can damage the body
urine	the liquid waste excreted by the kidneys

2 Living things in the environment

acid rain	rain that contains dissolved nitric oxides or sulphur dioxide; these compounds make the rain acidic
air pollution	air containing smoke and other harmful particles
deforestation	the removal of trees by humans

Remember:

Use these words when you discuss the topics in the unit so that learners become familiar with them.

endangered	plants or animals that have decreased in number
environment	the natural world
extinct	plants or animals that no longer exist
food chains	a way to describe the feeding relationship between plants and animals
habitat	the natural home of a plant or animal
pH	a measure of the amount of acid in a liquid
pollutants	substances that cause pollution
predator	a consumer that eats other animals
prey	animals that are eaten by other animals
producers	plants that produce energy from sunlight
species	a particular type of plant or animal

3 Material changes

dissolve	when a substance, often a solid, mixes with a liquid and becomes part of the liquid
mixture	two or more different substances mixed together that are not chemically joined
particle	a small part of something
rate	how fast something happens
saturated	unable to hold any more, e.g. a sponge is saturated when it cannot absorb any more water
scientific model	used by scientists to explain how and why something happens
separate	divide or split something into different parts
solute	the material that is dissolved.
solutions	mixtures of one substance in another, where the dissolved substance can no longer be seen
solvent	the liquid in which a solute dissolves

4 Forces and motion

balanced (forces)	when two forces acting in opposite directions on an object are the same size
drag	the name for friction in liquids and air
forcemeter	an instrument used to measure the size of forces
friction	a force between two objects that tries to stop them sliding past each other
pattern	when the results of an investigation show a regular or predictable change
tread	the thickness and pattern of lines on the sole of a shoe
unbalanced (forces)	when two or more forces acting in opposite directions on an object are not the same size
work	the amount of energy transferred when a force makes an object move

5 Electrical conductors and insulators

circuit diagram	a picture of a circuit that uses symbols to represent components
clamp	large alligator clips for connecting to terminals of a battery
conductor	a material that allows electricity to pass through it
current	the flow of electricity
elements	substances that exist in a natural state, such as gold or oxygen
insulator	a material that does not allow electricity to pass through it
lightning	natural electricity in the sky
rechargeable	a battery that can be charged again when it goes flat
semiconductors	substances that can be an electrical conductor or an electrical insulator
terminals	connecting points to an electric circuit
volts	the unit of measurement of the strength of electricity